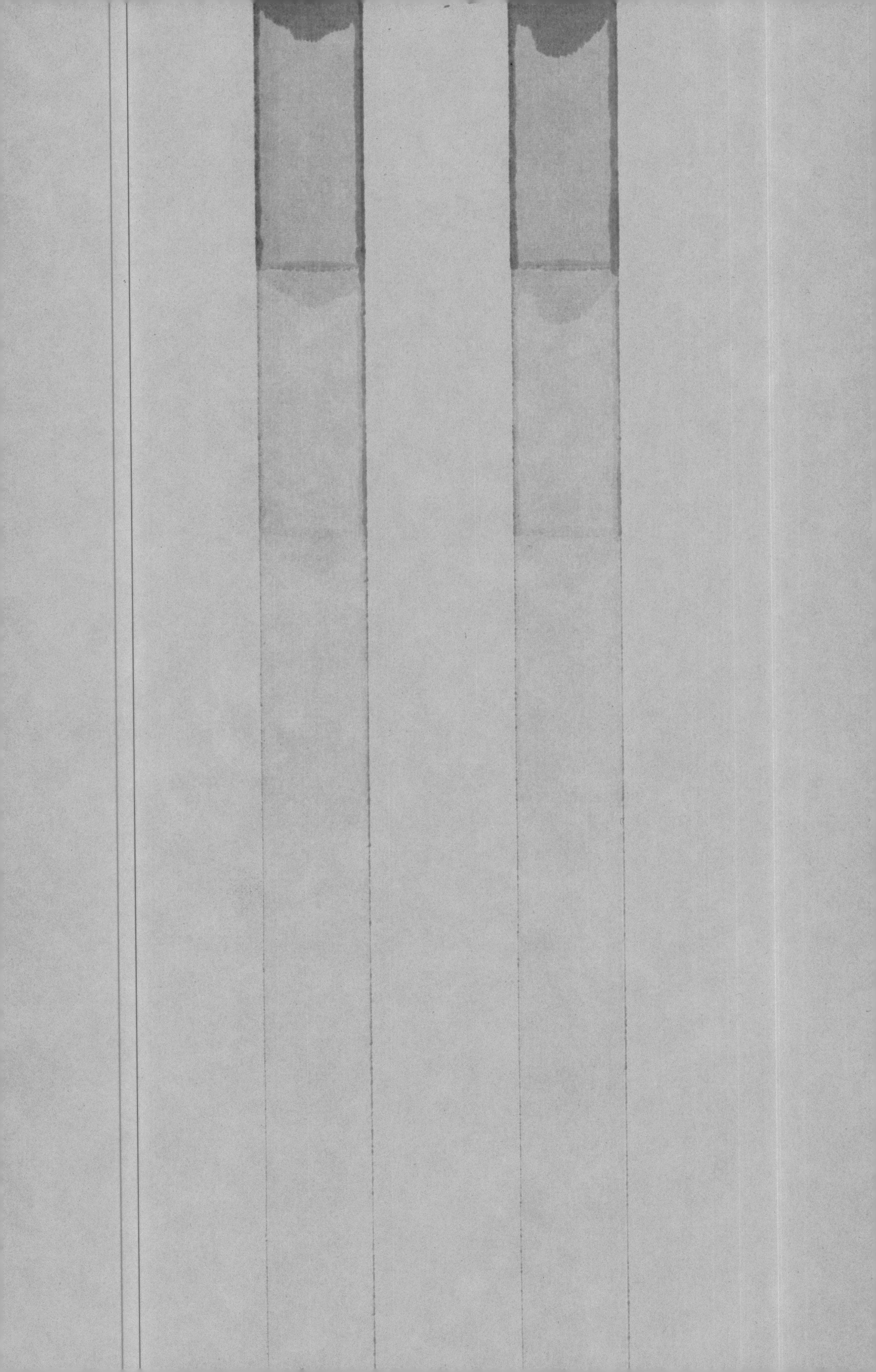

An Artist in Rome

To Judith,
with admiration,
Best, Adam
2/17/17

AN ARTIST IN ROME

Poems by

JOHN TAGLIABUE

Inspired by the Paintings of

ADAM VAN DOREN

KELLY-WINTERTON PRESS

ISBN 978-0-615-29226-7

When you are at Rome, do as you see.

— Cervantes

A. Van Doren

PREFACE

From the time I met the poet John Tagliabue in 1990, we shared a lively correspondence for the next fifteen years. He wrote the lion's share of the letters, and always included a cornucopia of inspired musings from his stream of consciousness: poems, quotations from famous writers, essays by friends and family, photos and clippings about art and literature.

I recently discovered that John had a more intense connection with my grandfather, the Pulitzer Prize poet and professor Mark Van Doren. John studied with him at Columbia in the 1940's. They remained friends for a long time afterward. My grandfather was moved to write about his former student: "He walks in the first mist, the one/ Before creation rested. He is affection/Not yet distilled, distinct; incapable of dying."

In preparation for a monograph on my artwork in 2006, John was asked if he might contribute a single poem in response to my paintings of Italy, where he was born. John, in a burst of enthusiasm and profound generosity, sent forty eight poems. "Much was written by whim and by wonder," he wrote to me, referring to these poems, "and Aristotle said 'wonder is the beginning of philosophy'. . . . I like spontaneity, exuberance, urgency, freshness. I let your paintings get me going."

The poems arrived too late for that publication, and John died shortly thereafter. This volume, which you now hold in your hands, is an attempt to fulfill what John so eagerly began. I am honored to have been a small part of it.

A. V. D.

AN APPRECIATION OF JOHN TAGLIABUE'S POEMS OF CELEBRATION

I don't know that John was born to be a poet. I think he could have become a dancer. He loved to dance, loved to dance in a ritualistic sort of way (at least on the occasions I saw him dance), and there is a sense of dance in much of his poetry. But he became a poet; and what a poet! One of his late poems mentions his "ten thousand" poems. Ten thousand? Multiply a single poem a day by seventy years of writing. What John was born to be was a celebrator. In this present volume you have him celebrating Adam Van Doren, Adam's paintings, the buildings that were Adam's subjects. A bit of John himself amazed and dazed by Adam, watercolor, sun, buildings, and the great builders of Italian civilization.

Here are five lines of celebration from his first volume, *Poems*. He may have been nineteen or twenty when he wrote them.

> The lady bug in her shell of beauty
> Speaks of the grandeur of God
> Of the varied colors and love of the cosmos
> In her small darkness she contains all secrets
> In her walking all poems

Anyone who knows John's poetry would know these words were his. Free verse, yes; easy verse, yes; most especially celebratory verse. Surrounding John at that time and later were other poets a little older, a little younger, writing very dense verse into which they themselves disappeared, others writings fraught poems about their own deeply troubled lives, others preoccupied with a world gone wrong or a world brutal from the start. John instead saw this lady bug who was beautiful and connected to grander objects of beauty in the colorful cosmos; and she possessed secrets of sexuality from which might spring love. Is there then no exaggeration in John's celebration except in the last line? Surely the lady bug was not a walking *Divine Comedy*! What John knew, though, was that many of his poems came to him as he walked. I walk, therefore I write. He must have been pleased to have the lady bug anticipate the writing of verse in this cosmos of secrets.

The terms to which John celebrated the lady bug can be found explicitly or implicitly in one or another of his Van Doren poems. John's celebrations are rarely if ever things in themselves. He wrote of things connected, for his celebrating vision was of a connected, living world. The poems of his first volume give us John already mature in style and substance, present in his work as he believed every real artist had to be. Inevitably one of his Van Doren poems suggests that Adam is sitting in his watercolors almost grand and invisible like God or an elephant.

There were uncounted sorts, variation, and heights of celebration. John has a late poem entitled "Saying Good-bye to 2 Retiring Assistants." They have gone around the world with him for many years, keeping in the background, always ready to help him. They are two molar teeth that he has to have extracted. The poem's closing words are "thank you." Another late poem begins "How many woodpeckers have I been for how many years." He is thinking of himself hitting typewriter keys, and he thinks Paderewski, the greatly famous pianist of his youth, could not have been more faithful at the piano than he was at his typewriter keyboard "stirring the alphabet into action." John has another poem celebrating the typewriter he is relinquishing in favour of an electronic typewriter. He says, "I have to give you up Smith Corona Galaxie Deluxe..." He must have been delighted that the typewriter itself bore the high words "corona" and "galaxy" for its modest celebration.

Among John's many wonderful poems of celebration are two I hold in special affection. The first is from *The Buddha Uproar*, 1970, and is beyond words to describe except with the poem in view.

You Can Go Very Far at That

The 1st time I learned to spell elephant I was transported,
The elephant thanked me,
I rode on him until I could spell India and Hindu and
"do you love?"

again the elephant answered yes and this time with a
chorus of tigers,
soon I was able to spell Blake and forests and the world
increased in wonder,
I didn't want to stop riding, it was great to be up there
And I was really dressed up
And there were festivals in every village that I entered.
When I opened a book birds flew out
Or rabbits came out of a word.
Then I saw a procession of elephants and even the Buddha.

This must be one of John's poems that his wife Grace says arrived by magic. It deals in magic, that of unforetellable life: learning to spell, learning the meanings of words and civilizations, learning love and great authors, learning riches at every turn, some sort of heaven and god. The poem is also a lovely serio-comic celebration of John himself in ecstasy, in triumphant progress, really dressed up for festivals, a suitable author. The title says the reader can go far too. I suspect that John could not have written such a poem as this until he had lived in India. I think he was not altogether easy with Christian deities; earthy Indian deities were more his sort. I never asked him.

The other poem is entitled "Though You Were Expecting It You Were Surprised". And John means you too again. He (though he doesn't use "I") is at an Italian railway station and sees a "short dark plump woman", "a black adolescent", a "thin woman with glasses who might be a middle-aged school teacher", a "burly guy with a plaid shirt" along with "red baseball cap" and "three short Sicilian women". He supposes that they all could sing "like songbirds in olive trees" and in single moment could . . .

read your mind as if it
were a musical score and
Obeying your Impulse
All together began
To Sing!

Perhaps John thought such celebration might save us.

James Hepburn
Amberley, England

LETTER FROM THE ACADEMY

Thy very weeds are beautiful, thy wreck a glory . . .
—Lord Byron

Molten blue, radiant ochres, burnt sienna and ultramarine. It is Rome in July. The sun, rising regal above the Palatine, casts deep, sumptuous shadows like Caravaggio. The Baroque sky, iridescent, cloudless, spreads over the temples like the sea.

In the summer of 2004, as a Visiting Artist at the American Academy in Rome, I set out to paint as much of the City as I could. It was presumptuous, perhaps foolhardy. To begin with, the weather was unusually hot. I was determined to work outdoors, however, and I adapted to the heat. Around me, tourists baked in the sun on dry, dusty streets, withering under the shrill drone of endless mopeds.

I was driven by my love of old buildings; the more ancient, the more enchanting. I suspect Brabazon, Corot and Turner had similar feelings. It was their representations of Italian ruins that lured me here. On my first day, I settled near the Colosseum. I unfolded my easel, took out my paints, and began my adventure. (Ironically, I could have worked at my Academy studio, where it was cool and comfortable, but I preferred *in situ*).

History in Rome is everywhere—and nowhere. The City is definitively ancient. New buildings are rare. When new structures are built, they seem to take forever, inhibited by strikes and siestas. Rome is not hospitable to developers, but to tourists and artists it is an inspiration. An observer must look closely to discover all the remnants of this historic empire— once stretching as far as Britain and Africa—because there is relatively little left. I was aware of some of the City's past; and it was startling to realize that the Forum, once the center of the known world, served as a cattle pasture during the Middle Ages. Centuries passed before it was exhumed. Mussolini dug the biggest holes; archeaologists are still digging. What survives is stained with soot and graffiti, but the design, the monuments of art, continue to remind us of the grandeur that was Rome.

I studied architecture in college, and I was familiar with the distinctions between a façade and a foundation. Among the most memorable lessons I learned was that the Romans invented the arch, a rare idea they didn't copy from the Greeks. This piqued my interest in all things curved: bridges, vaults and cupolas. Readings of Vitruvius demystified architraves, pediments, balustrades, aediculae, and pilasters (and how to pronounce them). Alberti distinguished the Corinthian from the Composite, the Doric from the Tuscan.

So many of the familiar scenes of Rome are perpetuated by postcard views, but I was determined to paint the Spanish Steps, the Pantheon, Trajan's Market and the churches of Borromini. It didn't discourage me that I was joining a large and distinguished company. *Veduti*, or views, were favorites of collectors throughout the 18th and 19th centuries, and many of the masters staked their reputations on them. Hubert Robert was one of the best, and I had pored over his landscapes at the Metropolitan Museum in New York. Thomas Jones was another. He deftly captured the City's palette and used grays beautifully. Undaunted by the artists whom I so greatly admired, I settled in to paint my own Rome.

I experimented with methods of watercolor that originated from oil painting. I prepared my Arches paper the night before with elaborate washes of color, using fat Chinese brushes to cover the surface completely. After establishing the "ground", or background, I carefully laid in the highlights. Gouache, or "body color" as the English called it, worked best for this effect. An advantage in Rome was that washes dried quickly in the sun, and didn't buckle the paper. Turner was a master at this, and his copious sketchbooks provide a legacy of this technique.

The painting of ruins presented a challenge. I could sketch and was experienced in rendering perspective, but crumbling masonry was like painting lasagna. There was no way to control the lines. I intuitively painted what I saw, with colors that seemed appropriate to my eye. The Baths of Caracalla were a great exercise. Weathered like worn cliffs, their huge, craggy walls had a strange beauty. Dwarfed next to them, I squinted, and viewed their ragged, distorted profile as an abstraction— a form in and of itself. I opted for the picturesque, adding overhanging weeds and moss, as Piranesi would have done. The rich patina was what I was after, and I liked the texture it contributed to the picture.

When I returned to my studio at the Academy, late in the afternoons, I was often exhausted from the long walk up Janiculum hill. I pinned my pictures to the wall and studied them. I was resistant of being too self –critical. It seemed to me I should first feast on fresh pasta and wine before revisiting my art. On to another day: again the white hot sunrise, the temple front— but always the opportunity to be inspired by the light of Rome.

Adam Van Doren
Rome

Active Extensions of Baroque Influenced Buildings, Desire and Light

Add
some flags to it
and wind and ardor
and the creative Venture of your Appreciation,
Invent, Add to the Bulge, the Bulk, the Bernini
            Exuberance of
a Building, Italian Operatic, Energetic Architecture;
            the Protruding
Curved Balconies of Extensions. To what Extent
            are you
Exaggerating or Celebrating Sturdiness and
            Stone and
            Desire?

up and down, in and out, one is faithful to the feel of
things, sculpture for the iconography
of Light and Dark

Cove and
an alcove and a cave,
a natural chapel, weeds, and from the very
old wall more weeds and words and flowers grow;
those unique countless builders through the centuries
insisted on indentations, insistencies concerning grottoes,
chapels, eroded, time sculptured as they may be, more and more
urgent ones needed to make indentations, curves, remarks for
the hands, so thousands of sculptors and architects
appeared upon the wide undulating Roman scene,
chiaroscuro, more chiaroscuro, texture for
philosophy and hands to explore,
sensational explorations,
all parts of the
body and faith

Theologies . . . . . and drowsiness . . . . . and awakenings . . . . change

Your clouds change,
your thoughts change,
your prayers change. . . . . above many Roman domes

some very large domes. . . . . some very small

some very large clouds. . . . . some small

at that. . . . . and don't forget also

the cherubs change. . . . . the lovers change their positions . . . also
the thoughts of people inside churches change,

the churches somewhat change

Blake: "Exuberance is beauty";
Adam Van Doren Showing Doors and Skies

The mountain
has risen, O yes, see its ample breast,
Rome is generous, faith has moved mountains,
the Sun Also Rises whether it is in Spain, Italy,
  New York City,
Anywhere in Due Time, give it time, give it your
  glorification
energy exuberance architecture, Blake and Bernini
  can Assist,
mountains, domes, suns loom large, sunsets
  add wide
splendor to the skies, exuberance and expanses
  and suns
are lavish joys. In Time Make a
  Church of
  All This.

Endurance Watercolors Sunlight

Take a Turn towards Turner or
        a
Burning Ardor of Bernini, Amass Sunsets,
        amass
Roman legions, columns of showing off, empires
        of hope
peace   power   where Italian endurance and sunlight
        are
Expressed.   Art has something to do with juice
        and Joy.

Of course we are in Rome and when in concord in recurring home

Roman colonnade, aubade, and serenade, made us accountable
for repetitions of
grandeur; this included reflections concerning mighty
columns and changing
sunlight; also we heard chords of music and were in accord
with some harmonies
heard by Plato, Marcus Aurelius, Emerson of Concord, some
outstanding calm.
Strongest musicians, light green of springtime and glowing
mild gold of old age.
Plus pleasing confidence as in Adam's watercolors,
reflections. Continuing
Genesis of this kind can be Accompanied by Fountains
of Enthusiasm.

Magnanimous Verdi and Monteverdi and Bernini,
not bourgeois (which for me means meagerness of feeling)
but instead grand suitable for ROME

Interceding. . . . and did you hear all the prayers inside the seed?
I heard them,
they sounded like my whispering in order not to wake me
when I was three,
three and trinity. . . . did you hear the cascade inside the
rain drops while
fountains of Rome applauded? So many contraltos and contrasts
after all the
lovers left by the shadows of the plants and the accumulated
dormant operas
by those fountains - that even not mild Bernini felt that yet
another opulent
statue should be made; so he and assistants proceeded; ROME
is not meager

Mark Van Doren, Adam's grandfather, Donald Keene later reported had "mentioned once in class in connection with some passage in St. Augustine that no action was more specifically human than to praise."

You will wake and
amazed see this Dome of a certain Santa Maria and then
Another and so on to Another Santa Maria, they are Magnificent,
there are Many, and you can exercise your strength and hope and
hope and desire for Peace going from One to the Other (is this
like saying the rosary?), so many domes cupolas others, saints
protectors, so many nameless mysteries, so we go from one to
another contributing to the City of Glory Imagining names
honoring architecture or prayers, practicing praise for
all this and more, making poems and paintings art
watercolors, Santa Maria piena di Grazia,
notebooks, memories, glowing rich with
praise. So continue to Praise raise
the Domes, busy dizzy visitor
with Glory.

A

Large
light
greenish
Niche

or
a
little
itch

can
entertain

Miracles With the Evasive

Don't think these bulky heavy often Very Magnificent
buildings
aren't evasive they disappear you close
your eyes you temporarily forget

these stupendous buildings with altars heavy crucifixes
Mosaics of the best designed most beautiful
colors the Queen of Heaven Crowning the Son
or the Dazzled Son Crowning the Mother

if a Child throws a Bernini church like a pebble into a pond
if he and the
Other One

say to It RISE it will like Him RISE

you will all be dazzled then a few
weeks or many months later
It May Seem to Disappear and you will
be like Empty Spaces
in the universe

that Child going to bed or Awaking with

you can after all tell the
universe what to do

To touch upon you lightly,
Eternal City, fragile beloved one,
serves us right

I fell asleep
inside a building of colors and songs after the rain,
so much love of this leaf that leaf this dome that dome
this reflection this crescendo this descending of a sightful
pleasure insightful pleasure a treasure 7 hills of Rome
countless windows countless celebrations of you my
love's different aspects

Certo, la città è bella

O, I did a lot a lot
of walking, I took refuge in a chapel of yours,
on a park bench, in front of a canvas, the city was my campus,
my education of broad beauty, higher learning, its houses' walls,
their colors all pleasing instructors; I asked you to pray
by looking, by saluting, by walking, by
Italian talking.

in	out
darkness	light
erosion	reflection
wetness	dryness
chiaroscuro	texture
facade's	entertainment

The book of changes,
the watercolors of change,
an exchange of salutations

Every breath is original,
every inspiration expiration, freshness is all;
the special quality of mercy, it droppeth as the
gentle
rain from heaven or the needed watercolor brushstroke
by the
artist in love with this place or face; let it
gently
refresh your memory and novelty; you are breathing;
you are
travelling, you are changing!

Also instances and instincts of brush strokes

These experts
these precisionists
flighty at different speeds and
undulations
know exactly how to land on a branch.
Know how
to ascend in air, alone or with
flighty
companions. Some even sing. All miraculous
which brings
us joy, variations, the words or birds.

A Van Doren

Warm Expansive Education and hours of rest

Lintels, portals, balconies
touched by light and green thoughts in at times
        green shade,
baked by strong warmth of Roman summer sun,
        many summers
many expansive nights, and stars seem to be teaching the
        ETERNAL CITY;
darkness and vastness profound for centuries of nights; but
        during the
Summer Day we are in a daze Wandering Wondering.

A Glowing Concern Responsive

The Sky
and large Roman Dome
were Together asked Where did
you go to Get that Glow? the answer slowly came:
Show your   Faith   Hope   Charity   Ardor   and you will   Know.

VAST and CHANGING Intimacy which is Impressive

Light on your various buildings, some with
 columns, porticoes,
changing light from the distant Impressive
 Slow Powerful Sun,
on varieties of Sturdy Grand Buildings. I see you as
 varied conversations,
not of the human trivial kind, interesting intense as
 they can sometimes be;
I see, hear, you in not paraphrasable grandeur.
 Wallace Stevens said
"The poem is the poem and not the paraphrase of the poem."
 I not only hear you
and carry you in my influences but I wonder about grand
 quiet subtle you.
You seem to quietly rest there on walls, on steps, and
 columns, perfectly
Composed, a grandeur of unanxious success, restful,
 unweighable as
a thoughtful elephant, you capable of becoming
 invisible, vast
and capable of disappearing, vast intimacy
 without arguments.

Nobility and strength awareness,
at rest

Time for a while to close your eyes, to rest in almost
darkness, fertility
resting, after a day or centuries of accomplishment, activity,
soft mild
warm darkness, the whole warm vital body in repose. There
arose in us
satisfaction thinking of those temples to the gods, goddesses,
emperors; those
mighty marble well formed columns in the dark. Accomplished,
monumental at
that. The complete satisfied body aware of the potential,
self-and-empire
aware, at rest.

A relatively small Roman church quiet in the dark

A relatively small Roman church quiet in the dark,
and a sarcastic Italian aunt of mine in the almost dark making
lace in her old age
indoors, fine lace, secret place, bemused, in love with me since
my childhood and
the secluded shadowy small church for centuries protecting
thoughts for me,
increasing the powers of prayers by me; tiny church like the nest
for a sparrow in
the dark; do not, do not, spare me any of your mosaic and
interior golden dreams,
crucifixion or Easter, amuse me with your limitations; sarcastic
quiet patient instinctive
proceeding aunt; or are you a mystic ant in the centuries'
darkness? what are those
angels saying and sounding off with their trophies and trumpets?
I thank you
for teaching me the untranslatable vows, for teaching me to bow.

hour
every
it
remember
or
hear
or
see
we
if
health
sound
and
hope
find
us
help
can
tower
bell
a
and
bell
a
and
hope
hope
I

To be read listening and ascending

I came   I saw   I prayed   I hope

Heavy columns strong almost splurging uprising sensual
ennobling sheltering and extending arches
people going to Pray know what is Indicative and Cooperative with
Almighty City of Cæsar and Hadrian and
undecipherable Popes and all
complex mysterious unreducible people
populations of ROME populations of
seekers from all over the world
millions said PAX ROMANA
will there ever be Peace ? we go to
pray for that

Paintings by Adam Van Doren

1
Roman Aqueduct, 2004, oil on canvas, 14 x 11 in.

2
The Academy Studio, Rome, 2004, watercolor on wove paper, 23 x 14 in.

3
Villa at Frascati, 2004, oil on canvas, 24 x 18 in.

4
Church of Santa Maria in Montesanto, 2004, watercolor on wove paper, 23 x 14 in.

5
Villa with Orange Window, 2005, oil on canvas, 24 x 18 in.

6
Theater Marcellus, 2004, watercolor on wove paper, 23 in x 14 in.

7
Caracalla Chiaroscuro, 2004, watercolor on wove paper, 14 x 20 in.

8
Renaissance Garden, 2005, oil on canvas, 11 x 14 in.

9
Temple in Forum, 2004, oil on canvas, 24 x 18 in.

10
Trees at Falconieri, 2004, oil on canvas, 16 x 20 in.

The Contributors

JOHN TAGLIABUE

John Tagliabue (1923–2006) was born in Cantu, Italy, in the house where his mother was raised. After study at Columbia University, he taught at the American University of Beirut, Lebanon, and later for over three decades at Bates College. He was awarded Fulbrights to teach in Indonesia, China, Japan and Italy; and he also lectured in Spain, Greece, Turkey and Brazil. His books include *Poems, A Japanese Journal, The Doorless Door, The Great Day*, and *New and Selected Poems, 1942–1997*. He and his wife Grace were married for almost 60 years.

ADAM VAN DOREN

Artist Adam Van Doren was educated at Columbia and the National Academy of Design. He has been a Visiting Artist at the American Academy in Rome and has taught at the Institute of Classical Architecture in New York. Van Doren has contributed essays to *The New York Times,* among other publications, and his paintings have been exhibited widely, including the National Portrait Gallery in Washington, D.C. An eponymous monograph of his watercolors was published by Hudson Hills Press in 2007. He has a studio in Manhattan.

JAMES HEPBURN

Critic James Hepburn took his degrees at Yale University and the University of Pennsylvania. Among his thirteen academic books *are The Author's Empty Purse and the Rise of the Literary Agent, Critic into Anti-Critic, A Book of Scattered Leaves*, and *Letters of Arnold Bennett*. His academic autobiography, *Confessions of an American Scholar*, appeared under the name Simon O'Toole. He has had seven plays produced, was a Guggenheim Fellow, and was Chairman of the English Department, Bates College from 1972–1987. He lives in West Sussex, England.

500 copies printed.
signed by the artist. Set in Requiem
types of the Hoefler Typefoundry, based on the
lettering of Ludovico Arrighi (c. 1475–1527)
of Vicenza, Italy. Printed on Oxford paper.
Designed by Jerry Kelly.

MMIX

Adam Van Doren